KAUAI

Bill and Diana Gleasner

TABLE OF CONTENTS

Mahalo to Jack Harter Of Jack Harter Helicopters
Who Made the Aerial Photographs Possible
Revised 1988 (4th printing)
ISBN 0-932596-03-7

The Oriental Publishing Company
P. O. Box 22162
Honolulu, Hawaii 96822

Distributed by Pacific Mercantile
P.O. Box 22156
Honolulu, Hawaii 96822   Phone: (808) 537-5404   537-5431

Printed by China Color Printing Co., Inc.
229, Pao Chiao Road, Hsintien
Taipei, Taiwan, R.O.C.

Other books in this series by Bill and Diana Gleasner include Maui Traveler's Guide, Oahu Traveler's Guide, Big Island Traveler's Guide and Hawaiian Gardens.

ALOHA

TOURS AND SIGHTSEEING TRIPS

Kauai has something for everyone — sightseeing tours, whale watching tours, bass fishing guides, snorkel and scuba trips, kayak river tours, hiking tours and even shopping tours. Check your telephone directory, consult with your hotel desk or with Activities Centers around the island.

The Hawaii Visitors Bureau, located on the second floor of the Lihue Plaza building, has a wealth of free information on every imaginable Kauai activity.

Na Pali Boat Tours and Sightseeing Trips

Adventures Unlimited Kauai	245-8766
Alana Lynn Too	245-7446
Aquatic Adventures	822-9768
Bali Hai Charters	826-9787
Blue Odyssey Adventures	826-9033
Bluewater Sailing	335-6440
Brennecke Ocean Sports	742-6570
Bubbles Below Inc	822-3841
Captain Andy's Sailing	822-7833
Captain Napali Boat Cruises	826-9696
Coastal Charters Kauai	822-7007
Fantasy Island Adventures	742-7288
Fantasy Island Boat Tours	742-6636
Gent-Lee Sightseeing Charters	245-7504
Hawaiian World	826-6558
The Hawaiian Z-Boat Company	826-9274
Island Adventure Inc	245-9662
Kauai Charter Boat Service	245-7502
Kauai Divers-Ramblin' Rose Charters	742-1580
Kauai Ocean Tours	826-7382
Lady Ann Cruises	245-8538
Lucky Lady Charters	822-7033
Magic Dragon Boat Charters	826-6623
Maritime Service Co.	742-9710
Momona Sailing Inc.	335-6092
Na Pali Adventures	826-6804
Na Pali Kai Tours Inc.	822-3553
Na Pali Zodiac	826-9371
Napali-Kauai Boat Charters	826-7254
Ocean Ventures	826-6151
Paradise Adventure Cruises	826-9999
Playtime Charters	335-5074
Ramblin' Rose Charters	826-7400
Sea Kauai	828-1488
Sea Sage Diving Center	822-3841
Seabreeze Charters	828-1285
Seascape Boat Tours	826-1111
Tide Rider Sailing Charters	742-6118
Tropic Aquatics	826-6088
Whitey's Na Pali Coast Cruises	826-9221

Na Pali Coast

HAWAIIAN WORDS AND PHRASES

alii — old royalty of Hawaii

aloha — hello, farewell, love

da kine — means just about anything, usually a positive type remark

hale — house

hana — work

haole — caucasian

heiau — ancient temple

holoku — formal dress with train

kai — sea

kamaaina — a person who was born in the islands or who has lived here a long time

kane — man

kapu — forbidden, keep out

kaukau — food

keiki — child

kokua — help

kona — south

lanai — porch

laulau — pork or beef cooked
 in ti leaves

lei — necklace, usually of flowers, seeds or nuts

lua — toilet

luau — feast

mahalo — thank you

makai — toward the sea

malihini — stranger

mauka — toward the mountains

muumuu — loose dress

ono — delicious

opu — stomach

pali — cliff

pau — done

pua — flower

poi — crushed taro root

puka — hole

pupu — hors d'oeuvres

wahine — female

wikiwiki — hurry

Kalalau Lookout

HELICOPTER TOURS AND HORSEBACK RIDING

There aren't any words that can possibly do justice to the experience of seeing Kauai by helicopter. So much of the island is wilderness and cannot be viewed in any other way.

Bali Hai Helicopter Tours	332-7331
Blue Pacific Helicopters	245-6807
Bruce Needham Helicopters	335-5009
Jack Harter Helicopters	245-3774
Kauai Helicopters	245-7403
Kenai Helicopters	245-8591
Menehune Helicopters Ltd.	245-7705
Na Pali Helicopters	245-6959
Niihau Helicopter Inc.	338-1234
Ohana Helicopters	245-3996
Papillon Helicopters Ltd.	826-6591
Rainbow Helicopters	245-4661
South Sea Helicopters	245-7781
Will Squyres Helicopter Service	245-7541
Island Helicopters Kauai	245-8588

Horseback Riding

Pooku Stables
P.O. Box 888
Hanalei, HI 96714
826-6777

Trail Riding, including beach and picnic rides, Hanalei Valley rides

CJM Country Stables
5598 Tapa
Koloa, HI 96756
245-6666

Horseback rides on the south shore. A three-hour ride on the beach with swimming and snorkeling. (One and two-hour rides also available).

LIHUE

This modernized plantation town is the government, business, transportation and cultural center of Kauai. It grew up around Lihue Plantation which was started in 1849 by three men who bought 1,875 acres of land from a local princess (for $9,350!) Today it is one of the largest sugar cane plantations in the state and one of the most modern in the world.

Kauai Museum — 4424 Rice Street across from the post office. The story of Kauai from its geological beginning to statehood is told in this two-building complex which also has changing art and cultural exhibits. (fee) The museum shop sells books, South Pacific imports and quality souvenirs.

Lutheran Church — look for the HVB marker near the sugar mill. The oldest Lutheran Church in Hawaii, built in 1883 to serve Kauai's German community.

NEAR LIHUE
(approximately two miles from town)

Kalapaki Beach has gentle surf and splendid view of Haupu, a peak of the Hoary Head mountains.

Westin Kauai — This sparkling new addition to Kauai's fine hotels includes two 18-hole golf courses designed by Jack Nicklaus and a spectacular 34,000-square-foot swimming pool which is the largest in the state.

Kukui Grove Shopping Center — At intersection of Nawiliwili Road and Kuhio Highway. Department stores, restaurants and specialty shops.

Nawiliwili Harbor The island's main docking facility for commercial ships. The harbor's huge bulk sugar plant holds 57,000 tons of raw sugar which is shipped direct to San Francisco for processing. You may see a cruise ship easing into the harbor or a fishing boat returning with a wonderful catch.

Menehune Garden The largest banyan tree on Kauai, native plants and herbs. (fee)

Menehune Fishpond The best example on Kauai of a prehistoric river-fed fishpond. Said to have been built in a single night by the Menehunes, a legendary race of two foot high people who were here before the Hawaiians. The pond which once belonged to chiefs and was taboo to all others is now a National Historic Site as well as a National Wildlife Preserve.

Grove Farm Homestead — Off Nawiliwili road (Highway 58). Historical museum of plantation life on Kauai. The original buildings and furnishings of one of the earliest plantations in Hawaii are carefully preserved after continuous use of more than a century. Unhurried, guided tours available Monday, Wednesday and Thursday. Advance reservations required. (245-3202). Fee.

Kilohana — The restored Wilcox Mansion recreates the 1930s era just outside Lihue on Kaumualii Highway (Rt. 5) The grounds feature tropical gardens, a working farm and a restoration of the old plantation workers' camp as well as interesting shops, demonstrations of Hawaiian crafts, carriage rides and restaurants. No admission charge for touring Kilohana. Personalized tours available for a slight fee. Call for information: 808-245-5608.

Kauai Community College — Across the road from Puhi. Note the metal sculpture at the entrance of this attactive complex.

Fishing, Hawaiian Style

Lutheran Church, Lihue

Waterfall on floor of Waialeale's Crater, world's wettest place.

KOLOA, POIPU and SPOUTING HORN
Via Rt. #50 and #52

Tree Tunnel — Eucalyptus trees arch over route 52, better known as the tree tunnel, which branches off main highway 50 on the way to Koloa, Poipu and Spouting Horn.

Koloa — Koloa, which means long cane, was at one time the center of activities on Kauai. The remains of the old chimney on the right as you enter town is all that remains of the mill from the first sugar plantation in Hawaii which was started here in 1835. Walking towards the old mill you will find different varieties of sugar cane grown in Hawaii and a sculpture depicting all the ethnic groups that contributed to the success of Hawaii's sugar industry.

The completely restored Old Koloa Town has kept all its charm while becoming a favorite place for shopping and browsing. An open-air jitney takes you around town and to Poipu Beaches at no charge.

Buddhist Temple — located at the eastern end of Koloa Town has been carefully restored, and the ornate altar can be seen from the entry.

St. Raphaels Church — Take Weliweli Road and then the right fork onto Hapa Road. Built in 1856, the church was surrounded by houses, stone walls and terraces. The ruins can still be seen.

A few miles south of Koloa the road divides in opposite directions along the beach. The intersection, once a thriving winter whaling port, is Koloa Landing. The road to the left goes to Poipu with its string of luxury hotels and the Poipu public recreation park and beach. The climate in this area is dry, the scenery photographable and the beaches among the best anywhere.

Plantation Gardens One of the world's important cacti collections is located next to the Plantation Gardens restaurant. (See section on gardens, page 29)

Poipu Beach — Poipu, one of the favorite swimming beaches of Kauai, has pavilions, tables, showers and a volleyball area. Children can play in a shallow protected swimming pond. Brennecke's Beach (to the left as you face the ocean) is considered one of the best body surfing beaches on the island. The point just beyond Brennecke's is where Kauai's last volcanic eruption occurred. The beach to the right of Poipu Park is good for board surfing when conditions are favorable.

Prince Kuhio Park — The Park on the right side of the road, the Prince's birthplace, has a monument dedicated to Prince Jonah Kuhio Kalanianaole who served as Hawaii's delegate to the United States Congress when Hawaii became a territory. Prince Kuhio was born of royal parentage in 1871.

Spouting Horn — Beyond the small harbor built for fishing boats is the horn, a natural sea geyser, which forms a spectacular fountain when the surf is up. To the left of Spouting Horn was once a much larger blowhole but in 1910 the Plantation owners dynamited it because the spray was killing the sugar cane. Today it's just a large puka (hole) in the lava.

Poipu Area

Tree Tunnel

Brennecke's Beach

Body Surfing at Brennecke's

South Shore

Spouting Horn

LIHUE TO HAENA
Via Rt. #56

Wailua Falls — Just outside Lihue, take the left branch of the road in Kapaia. Four miles inland are the falls, a lovely pool below and hala trees all around.

Hanamaulu — Originally populated by families of Portuguese descent who arrived on Kauai around 1878. Some of the original white-washed camp houses can be seen beyond the company store. Next to the post office is the Hanamaulu Cafe with a charming Japanese garden and teahouse.

Lydgate Park — Long beautiful beach with protected swimming areas for kids.

Wailua River — This is where the first migratory Tahitians landed about 1000 A.D. The coconut grove by the river mouth marks the remains of Kauai's City of Refuge, a sacred enclosure where tabu violators could escape the death sentence IF they could outrun their pursuers. The boat traffic on this, the largest navigable river in Hawaii, consists mostly of tourists taking the trip to the **Fern Grotto**, a prehistoric shelter bedecked with hanging tropical ferns.

Smith's Tropical Paradise — (See Garden Section page 29)

Coconut Grove — Turn left just beyond the bridge onto route 580, On your right is one of the state's largest coconut groves. Once the domain of Kauai's last Queen, it is now the grounds of the Coco Palms Hotel.

Wailua River State Park — On route 580 opposite the coconut grove is the Holoholoku Heiau. (Heiaus are sacred temples built by the Hawaiians). In the left rear corner is a large stone which was once used for human sacrifices. The stairs to the right lead to a quaint Japanese cemetery.

Opaekaa Falls — At the crest of the hill on 580 you can view these sparkling falls, the Wailua River (just across the road from the falls) and the Pacific Ocean (from the Bell Stones which were struck in ancient times to announce royal births.)

Kamokila Hawaiian Village — Reconstructed native Hawaiian village across from Opaekaa Falls. One of the few opportunities for the traveler to see and participate in early Hawaiian crafts and other aspects of daily living. Charge.

The Market Place — Shopping complex on route 56 with attractive grounds and fountains. Free hula show every Thursday, Friday and Saturday at 4 p.m.

Kapaa — The main road is lined with interesting 19th century wooden buildings, many with balconies. The Japanese Monument in Kapaa town park, buried in 1943 because of wartime community pressure, was resurrected in 1987 to its original site in the park. During the 1900s the Japanese community here raised funds and sent money to Japan to help in the war against Russia. After the war, Japan sent back the money asking that it be used to build a monument of appreciation for Kauai's Japanese community.

Waipahee Falls and Slide — In Kealia take the road off to the left by the corral, go uphill to the Spaulding Monument and continue on a dirt cane road. This natural rock slide is the remnant of a lava tube where swimmers can shoot into a pool of fresh water. The road and the swimming become very dangerous in rainy weather.

LIHUE TO HAENA (con't)

Kilauea Lighthouse – Superb views in every direction of the rugged coastline. Boobies, shearwaters and terns nest in the bluff. The lighthouse's unique 12 foot clam shell lens is the largest of its type in the world.

Princeville – A recreational resort community and golf course overlooking the ocean and Hanalei Bay. Also a plantation style shopping center for pleasant browsing.

Hanalei Valley – A serene setting of taro patches and vegetable farms overseen by magnificent mountains ribboned by silver waterfalls.

Waioli Mission House – A National Historic Site built and furnished with materials the missionaries brought around Cape Horn. Guided tour. No reservations required. Fee.

Hanalei Bay – A favorite anchorage for yachts and sailboats, this crescent-shaped bay has a picturesque pier and fine sandy beaches.

Lumahai – The first beach past Hanalei, Lumahai was the nurse's beach in the movie South Pacific. Don't spare the film. You'll not find a lovelier beach anywhere.

Haena Beach Park – Camping and picnicking. One of the best places on Kauai to find puka shells.

Manini-holo Dry Cave – Across the road from the park. Stroll back inside this lava tube and think how much effort the Menehunes put into digging it.

Waikanaloa Wet Cave – Marked by the HVB sign, the cave is a short walk up a trail. Pele dug this cave for her lover but moved on quickly when it filled with fresh water.

Ke'e Beach – The end of the road on the North Shore. Reef-protected swimming in an idyllic setting that includes tall cliffs, palms and ironwoods rimming the beach. Once the site of Laka's temple (the goddess of the hula.)

Na Pali Coast – Fifteen miles of the world's most beautiful coastline begins at Haena and ends at Polihale State Park.

Haena

Kilauea Cliffs

Hanalei Bay

Waioli Mission House

Taro Farmer

Hanalei Valley

Haena Beach Park

Hanalei Valley

Haena Beach Park

Torch Lighting, Coco Palms

Haena Sunset

LIHUE TO POLIHALE
Via Rt. #50

Kukuiolono Park — South of Kalaheo. A superb setting with great views of the sea. Formerly the private estate of sugar plantation owner Walter McBryde, Kukuiolono has a tranquil Japanese garden, a collection of Hawaiian legendary stones and a nine hole golf course.

Pacific Tropical Botanical Garden (See Garden Section, page 29)

Olu Pua (See Garden Section, page 29)

Hanapepe Valley — Stop at the overlook for views of taro patches and farm plots below, red canyon walls and a distant waterfall.

Hanapepe — An open town (not owned by the plantation) in the early sugar years, this rowdy community has become staid and sleepy. Presently there is a strong community effort to preserve and rejuvenate the old buildings. Well worth a drive-through.

Salt Pond — Just past Hanapepe turn left on route H 543 and then take the first right past the veteran's cemetery. During the summer months you may see salt being dried in shallow pans in the old Hawaiian way.

Burns Field — The first airfield on the west side of Kauai. Used for some helicopter flights and a favorite weekend place for ultralight planes. Quite a colorful sight with the ocean as a backdrop.

Fort Elizabeth — Just before the Waimea River Bridge take the stairway and short trail toward the sea. This fort in the shape of a six pointed star was built by the Russians who had designs on Kauai in 1817.

Waimea — A memorial in the middle of town honors Capt. Cook's 1778 landing. Thanks to the Main Street Program, a self-help program that has involved the west side community, the area is a delightful stop en route to Kokee. Stop at the library for a copy of the selfguided walking tour of Waimea. A leisurely stroll past these historical buildings, some dated as early as 1828, will give you a feeling for the early life in Waimea.

Menehune Ditch — Turn right at the Big Save in Waimea. Drive approximately two miles. Once an impressive aqueduct, this watercourse is primarily of interest to the archeologist because of its flanged and fitted stones which pre-date the work of Polynesian stone masons. Across the road from the Menehune Ditch is the swinging bridge which is fun for the adventurous.

Waimea Canyon — A rift which has been eroded to a mile wide, ten miles long and up to 4,000 feet deep. The road up winds through forests of eucalyptus, silver oak and koa. Don't miss any of the lookouts. All are impressive. Be alert for wild goats on ledges below. In the morning the blues and greens dominate; in late afternoon the canyon walls are afire with reflected reds and golds.

Kokee State Park — Cool mountain country with plenty of trails for hikers which lead to the brink of Waimea Canyon, the edge of the Alakai swamp and points overlooking Na Pali Coast. You may get meals or rent cabins at Kokee Lodge. Be sure to stop in the museum next to the lodge for information on flora and fauna, petroglyphs, shells and the history of the area.

Kalalau Lookout — Up the road from Kokee Lodge. Absolutely outstanding. If it's foggy or rainy, be patient. You'll likely be rewarded with the world's best view which often includes a rainbow. This valley was the hideout of Koolau the Leper who garrisoned himself behind the knifelike ridges of Kalalau when the National Guard tried to forcefully relocate him to the Molokai Leper Colony. He hid in the valley with his wife and son until leprosy took his life.

Barking Sands — Named for huge sand dunes which supposedly go "woof" when you slide down them. Now a U.S. Naval installation.

Polihale State Park and Beach — One of the most impressive beaches anywhere, Polihale is a vast expanse of sand with a good view of Niihau (17½ miles off the coast of Kauai) and of the Na Pali cliffs which begin here and end in Haena. Picnic pavilion, camping facilities, showers and rest rooms. At times of high surf the swimming is dangerous due to strong rip tides.

Niihau — A private island owned by the Robinson family of Kauai. The last stronghold of pure Hawaiians where life is still lived in the age old ways.

Kauai Canyon Country

Hanapepe

Niihau in the sunset

Waimea Canyon

Heliconia

THE GARDENS OF THE GARDEN ISLAND

Plantation Gardens at Poipu is on the grounds of the Plantation Gardens Restaurant. This world famous collection of cacti and succulents is one of the oldest gardens on the island. The Moir family who started the garden in the 1930's put plantings around lava rock terraces and fireplaces saved from early Hawaiian days and used whaler's try-pots, Chinese grindstones and sugar millstones from more recent times. Bromeliads, orchids, night blooming cereus, water lilies and plumeria trees add color and variety to the desert plant scene.

Pacific Tropical Botanical Garden in Lawai is a research garden specializing in tropical plants. Started in 1970, the garden's emphasis on research and education is long overdue. Ninety per cent of the world's plants are found in the tropics, yet only ten per cent of all plant research has been devoted to them. The Botanical Garden is building impressive collections of rare and endangered plants along with tropical legumes, palms, coconut trees, breadfruit, ornamentals, vanillas, gingers and other spices. Limited tours, by reservation only, include the John Allerton estate with pools, statuary and gravity-fed fountains and water courses. (fee, 332-7361)

Olu Pua just beyond Kalaheo is several gardens in one. Originally part of a pineapple manager's estate, Olu Pua contains a jungle walk, an oriental garden, a palm garden, sunken garden, succulent garden, blue garden and a kaukau (food) garden. Visitors are given a printed map and may wander at their leisure. Open Monday, Wednesday and Friday for guided tours only. Call for times. 332-8182. Fee.

Smith's Tropical Paradise behind the Wailua Marina is located in the midst of highly-revered land which was once the domain of Hawaiian royalty. This garden specializes in native flowers and fruits as well as representing the cultures that make up present day Kauai. Tour guides explain the Polynesian and Filipino Villages and the Japanese Shrine. (fee) At night young islanders perform traditional dances of old Hawaii, Japan, Tahiti, China and the Philippines on a stage built over a lagoon. (fee) Free shuttle from Wailua Area Hotels and Condos. Reservations required for Luau, shuttle and show. 822-4654, 822-9599 or 822-3467.

Keahua Arboretum – a lovely walk by a mountain stream. Take Highway 580 (next to Coco Palms Hotel) and drive two miles past the University of Hawaii Experiment Station.

Awaawapuhi Trail – a 3¼ mile trail featuring many native plants that winds down a ridge separating Awaawapuhi from Nualolo Valley. Guide book is available from the Department of Land and Natural Resources located at the State Building.

Iliau Nature Loop – a short loop trail along the edge of Waimea canyon. Native plants are identified by wooden plaques. The trail is named for the Iliau, a relative of Maui's silversword. (See photo of Iliau on page 27).

Shimonishi Orchids in Hanapepe – An orchid lover's dream with 1600 varieties of orchids on display. Many may be purchased and shipped. Call 335-5562 for directions.

Smith's Tropical Paradise

Plantation Gardens

Pacific Tropical Botanical
Garden

Olu Pua

Lotus

Cup of Gold

Fun for Kids
or
Da Kine for Keikis

To See and Do

Nawiliwili Port Area – A submarine or naval destroyer might be docked. They often give free tours to the public.

Free Hula Show at the Marketplace – A colorful music and dance presentation for all ages. Thursday, Friday and Saturday afternoons at 4 p.m.

Small zoo at Coco Palms Resort – Not a complete Noah's Ark by any means but the monkeys are always glad to chatter at the "keikis".

Locomotive Day on second Tuesday of each month. Be at end of road behind Grove Farm office in Puhi by 9 a.m. to watch diminutive locomotives chug along a track once used to haul sugar cane. For more information call 245-3202.

Spouting Horn on the south shore and Kilauea on the north shore are excellent attention getters for the younger set. Should be on adult agendas as well.

Kauai Regional Library, 4344 Hardy Street, plus several branch libraries offer free children's films weekly. The Hawaiiana section has books on everything from surfing to ancient legends.

Torch Lighting Ceremonies – Evenings at Coco Palms Resort. Impressive for all. Check for time.

For Waterlovers

Lydgate – Protected lava pools and sandy beach. Good for beginning snorklers.

Poipu – Something for any age or ability including a specially well-protected pool for the very young in front of the pavilion area.

Tidepools – Hours of engrossing fun exploring tidal pools at the ocean's edge. Inexpensive nets and buckets can be purchased at the local hardware or fishing supply stores. You may have a budding marine biologist.

Eating

Island Food Musts

    Kauai Kookies
    Saimin (noodle soup)
    Barb-B-Q Meat Sticks
    Macadamia Nut Ice Cream
    Macadamia Nut Cookies (Tip Top Bakery)
    Portuguese Sweetbread (at any grocery)
    Lappert's Ice Cream

If you are getting pressure for good ole Mainland-style food, Lihue has McDonalds, Kentucky Fried Chicken, Pizza Hut, Burger King, Farrells, Wendys, Zippys and a Sizzler. Dairy Queens we scattered around the island also.

Shopping – Just for kids
  Hale Keiki, High as a Kite and The Sticker Store at the Marketplace
  Tutu's Kiddy Korner at Kilohana
  Tutu's Toy House at Kiahuna Shopping Village

Safe Beaches

The most popular and safest beaches are at Poipu, Kalapaki Hanalei by the pier, Wailua at the Kapaa end (stay away from the river end) and Haena at the end of the road on the north shore.

Undertows, strong currents and rip tides make swimming risky at Lumahai Bay, in front of the picnic pavilions at Hanalei and Haena and at Polihale State Park.

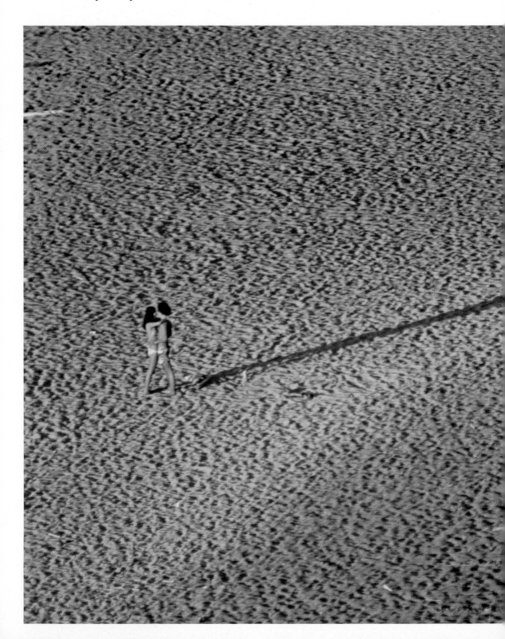

TENNIS

Public Courts
Lihue — Next to the Convention Hall
Kapaa — Little League Park in the middle of town
Koloa — Next to the fire station on Highway 52
Kalaheo — Kalaheo — Kalawai Park
Hanapepe — Near Hanapepe Pavilion
Waimea — Waimea High School

Hotel and Private Courts Open to the Public
Coco Palms Hotel — Wailua
Hanalei Bay Resort — Princeville
Sheraton Coconut Beach Hotel — Coconut Plantation
Kiahuna Beach and Tennis Resort — Poipu Beach
Princeville Tennis Courts — Princeville
Waiohai and Poipu Beach Hotels — Poipu Beach

Kiahuna Beach and Tennis Resort

GOLF

Westin Kauai —
  at Kalapaki Beach near Lihue
  Two 18 hole courses

Kukuiolono Golf Course
  Kukuiolono Park in Kalaheo
  9 holes

Princeville Makai Golf Course
  Princeville at Hanalei
  36 holes

Wailua Golf Course
  Wailua
  18 holes

Kiahuna Golf Course
  Poipu Beach
  18 holes

Kukuiolono Park

FISHING

Kauai offers fishermen outstanding opportunities for a bountiful catch. Many world record fish have been pulled over the transom off Na Pali coast. Albacore, bonito, Jack cravelle, barracuda, mahimahi (dolphin), marlin, ono and bonefish are found in abundance. Huge schools of yellowfin tuna grab bait in late spring with weights running up to 269 pounds.

Charters

Adventures Unlimited Kauai
Kuhio Hwy
245-8766

Kaulakahi
Kekaha
337-1806

Alana Lynn Too
Nawiliwili
245-7446

Lucky Lady Charters
Wailua
822-7033

Bass Guides of Kauai
Lihue
822-1405

Queensland Marine Corp.
Lihue
245-8455

Coastal Charters Kauai
Nawiliwili
822-7007

Seabreeze Sport Fishing
Anini
828-1285

Gent-Lee Fishing
Lihue
245-7504

Seascape Boat Tours
Lihue
245-1666

Hawaiian Z-Boat Co.
Hanalei
826-9274

Sport Fishing Kauai
Koloa
742-7013

Diving

Aquatics Kauai
Kapaa
822-9213

North Shore Bike, Cruise and Snorkel Inc.
Kapaa
822-1582

Dive Kauai
Kapaa
822-0452

Ocean Odyssey Dive Shop
Kapaa
822-9680

Fathom Five
Koloa
742-6991

Sea Sage Diving Center
Kapaa
822-3841

Kauai Divers
Koloa
742-1580

KALALU TRAIL
Na Pali Coast State Park

Whether you plan an extended pack trip or allow just a brief time for hiking, you should not miss an opportunity to stroll into old Hawaii along the ancient Kalalau Trail. This coastal trail traverses towering sea cliffs and lush valleys, dropping to sea level only at the beach-fronted valleys of Hanakapiai and Kalalau.

Kee Beach to Hanakapiai (2 miles – 1 hours) The trail begins at Ke'e Beach at the end of Highway 56. A ¼ mile walk will reward you with an excellent vista of Ke'e Beach and the reefs of the Haena coast. An even better view unfolds near the ½ mile trail marker. Two miles of hiking leads to Hanakapiai Valley, a sandy beach in summer but sometimes only a rocky shoreline in winter. From September to April the shoreline is extremely treacherous with strong surf and rip currents.

You may picnic at Hanakapiai Beach and, on two spur trails, explore the lush interior of Hanakapiai Valley. Hanakapiai Valley Loop Trail leads across ancient Hawaiian taro terraces, among huge mango trees and by the site of a small abandoned coffee mill. Hanakapiai Falls Trail, extending from the upper portion of the loop trail, leads to Hanakapiai Falls at the upper end of the valley. The first half of the falls trail is easy, but the upper portion is quite rugged. If the first stream crossing of the Falls Trail is difficult because of high water, the upper crossings will be impossible. The Hanakapiai Falls Trail should be attempted only during calm, clear water in the highlands, because of the danger of flash flooding in the upper narrow portion of the valley. There is also danger of falling rocks from the cliff in the area near the waterfall.

Hanakapiai to Hanakoa (4 miles – 2½ hours) Leaving Hanakapiai, the Kalalau Trail climbs abruptly and doesn't drop to sea level again for nine miles until it reaches Kalalau Beach. The trail crosses Hoolulu and Waiahuakua Valleys before reaching Hanakoa Valley. Hanakoa is a terraced valley once cultivated by the early Hawaiians. Exotic plant life has invaded and thickly covered the terraced areas. Hanakoa Shack is a state trail crew shelter open to backpackers when not being used by trail crews. Hanakoa Falls Trail (¾ mile in length) crosses ancient terraced areas and leads to Hanakoa Falls which cascades down the Pali at the rear of the east fork of the Hanakoa Valey.

Hanaokoa Valley to Kalalau Beach (5 miles – 3 hours) The trail continues along the rugged coastline which becomes more arid as you approach Kalalau. At the eastern slope of Kalalau Valley, there is a spectacular panorama of Kalalau Valley and Kalalau Beach. The trail crosses the valley near the shoreline until it reaches the beach. The camping area is located inland beneath the trees in front of the cliff. During the summer, campers may use caves west of the waterfall for shelter. Camping is not permitted along stream banks, near the stream mouth, or up in the valley. Do not walk along the base of steep cliffs because of the danger of falling rocks.

Kalalau Valley Trail (2 miles) leads inland to Big Pond, a scenic freshwater pool. Midway, the dense vegetation opens up providing a panoramic view of Kalalau Valley. The valley is particularly lush along the river bank, and you may come upon remnants of house sites used by Hawaiians who inhabited the valley until the late 1920s.

Camping Allowed at Hanakapiai, Hanakoa and Kalalau in designated areas. Camping permits are required as well as day use permits beyond Hanakapiai. A maximum of five nights allowed along the Na Pali Coast. No two consecutive nights at Hanakapiai or Hanakoa within the five nights. You may pick up permits at the State Parks Office in Lihue, Kauai, Monday to Friday (except holidays) from 8 to 4:15. For further information contact the Department of Land and Natural Resources, Division of State Parks, Outdoor Recreation and Historic Sites, State Building, Lihue, 3060 Eiwa and Hardy Streets (P.O. Box 1671), Lihue, Kauai, Hawaii 96766 (245-4444).

Warning! Boil or treat ALL water. Mountain climbing is extremely dangerous due to precipitous terrain and loose, crumbly soil. Flash floods are a real danger. Never cross a flooded stream. Wait for the water to recede. Swimming is not recommended. Unpredictable ocean currents have caused several drownings. Goat hunting is permitted in August and September (weekends and holidays) from Hanakoa to Kalalau. Safety Zone signs are posted. During these times confine hiking to main trails only. You are responsible for packing out all litter and trash.

Canoe racers leave Coco Palms Beach

Kalalau

Na Pali Coast

Na Pali Coast

Na Pali Coast

Weather

The north side of the island (the Hanalei area) where the mountains are closer to the coast receives the most rainfall, over 70 inches annually. Some sections along the south and southwest shores (the Poipu area and Barking Sands) have less than 20 inches of rain per year. Waialeale, a 5,075 foot mountain in the center of Kauai, is the world's rainiest spot with over forty feet per year.

Northeasterly trade winds keep the temperatures moderate — usually in the seventies — throughout the year with winter averaging 8 degrees below summer. The mountainous region is about 13 degrees cooler than Lihue, the record low being 27 degrees at Kokee.

Kona storms during the winter come from the south and usually bring moderate to heavy rains. The Hawaiians used to call them the "dying" winds and doctors today often find their waiting rooms fill up when the Kona winds are blowing.

Waialeale

Kauai's Past

Up from the sea came Kauai, rumbling and spewing bubbling lava from its volcanic core. The ocean, the winds and the rains took over, carving their masterpiece into a circular shape with sharply-ridged mountains, deep canyons and valleys. Over millions of years the final touches were added — waterfalls, rivers, lush greenery and white sand beaches. This, the most ancient island in the chain, was the first to cool down and concentrate on becoming a mature beauty.

The first Polynesians to land in Hawaii pulled their canoes onto the shore near the Wailua River, their incredible voyage across the ocean over at last. Later, another "first" landing was made when Captain James Cook stepped onto red Kauai earth in Waimea in 1778. From then on things changed rapidly for Kauaians. A bustling trade brought foreigners to buy and barter for fragrant sandalwood until the last tree was stripped from the mountains.

King Kamehameha, after conquering all the other islands, tried unsuccessfully to take Kauai. It wasn't until 1810 that the King of Kauai voluntarily submitted to all-island rule. Lifestyles changed drastically with the introduction of the missionaries' culture in 1820. During the 19th century there was a rivalry between the United States, Great Britain, France and Russia for control of the islands, but Hawaii managed to remain independent until 1898. In 1835 sugar cane growing began in Koloa and workers from many countries immigrated to work the fields. Sugar remained the economic mainstay of the islands for many years and is still an important source of income on Kauai. Annexation by the United States took place in 1900 and in 1959 Hawaii became a state.

Sugar on Kauai

Those first hardy Tahitians had sugarcane in their double-hulled canoes when they landed here in about the sixth century A.D.

Early Hawaiians planted it as a windbreak around their homes. They broke off sections to chew along the way when they set off on their travels.

Later, three New Englanders founded the first successful sugar plantation in 1835. From lands granted to them by King Kamehameha III, they harvested their first crop of two tons of raw sugar.

Today there are seven sugar companies on the island which produce about a fifth of Hawaii's total production. Between the island's year-round sunshine and the careful tending by sugar technologists, Kauai lands produce the highest yield of sugar per acre of any area in the world.

Cane on Kauai takes about two years to mature. After the harvest, replanting is usually done by machine although sometimes a mule is used to avoid injury to tender young plants.

Just before harvest, whole fields of cane are deliberately set on fire. This destroys unwanted leaves and other trash and does not affect the sugar content.

Practically all the operations of the sugar industry are mechanized so large groups are never seen working in the fields. Employees are the highest paid agricultural workers in the world today.

Sugar has determined the way Kauai has used much of its land. With the world running low on verdant spaces, sugar is keeping the Garden Island green.

Sugar Cane Fields

Burning The Cane Fields Before Harvest

Hotels in Lihue

Ahana Motel Apartments 3115 Akahi St.	20 units 245-2206
Hale Lihue Motel 2931 Kalena St.	18 units 245-3151
Hale Pumehana P.O. Box 709	16 units 245-2106
Motel Lani P.O. Box 535	10 units 245-2965
Tip Top Motel 3173 Akahi St.	34 units 245-2333

Hotels Near Lihue

Banyan Harbor Resort 4311 Wilcox Road Lihue, HI 96766	8 units 245-7333
Kauai Hilton and Beach Villas 4331 Kauai Beach Drive Lihue, HI 96766	500 units 245-1955
The Westin Hotel Lihue, HI 96766	850 units 245-5050
Ocean View Motel Nawiliwili R.R. 1, Box 192 Lihue, HI 96766	16 units 245-6345

Hotels in Wailua

Coco Palms Hotel P.O. Box 631 Lihue, HI 96766	420 units 822-4921
Kaha Lani Condominium RR 1, Box 500 Lihue, HI 96766	74 units 822-9331
Kapaa Sands R.R. 1, Box 3-H Kapaa, HI 96746	22 units 822-4901

| Kauai Resort Hotel | 242 units |
| Wailua, HI 96766 | 245-3931 |

Kauai Sands Hotel	176 units
R.R. 1, Box 4-K	822-4951
Kapaa, Kauai, HI 96746	

Lae Nani Condominium	39 units
410 Papaloa Road	822-4938
Kapaa, HI 96746	

| Wailua Bay View Apartments | 22 units |
| Wailua, HI 96766 | 822-3651 |

Hotels in Waipouli

Sheraton Coconut Beach Hotel	311 units
Coconut Plantation	822-3455
Kapaa, HI 96746	

Islander on the Beach	199 units
P.O. Box 68	822-7417
Kapaa, HI 96746	

Kapaa Shore	18 units
4-0900 Kuhio Highway	822-3751
Kapaa, HI 96746	

Kauai Beach Boy	243 units
Waipouli Beach	822-3441
Kapaa, HI 96746	

Kauai Kailani Apartments	56 units
856 Kuhio Highway	822-3391
Kapaa, HI 96746	

| Plantation Hale Resort | 160 units |
| Waipouli, HI 96746 | 822-4941 |

Hotels in Kapaa

Hotel Coral Reef	26 units
1516 Kuhio Highway	822-4481
Kapaa, HI 96746	

Pono Kai Resort	68 units
4-1250 Kuhio Hwy.	822-9831
Kapaa, HI 96746	

Hotels — Princeville at Hanalei

Alii Kai	59 units
P.O. Box 310	826-9921
Hanalei, HI 96714	
Hanalei Bay Resort	120 units
P.O. Box 220	826-6522
Hanalei, HI 96714	
Pali Ke Kua	70 units
P.O. Box 121	531-7595
Hanalei, HI 96714	
The Makai Club at Princeville	20 units
P.O. Box 121	826-3820
Hanalei, HI 96714	
Sheraton Princeville	300 rooms
Princeville, HI 96722	826-9644
SeaLodge	36 units
P.O. Box 121	826-6751
Hanalei, HI 96714	

Hotels — Hanalei to Haena

Cliffs at Princeville	80 units
P.O. Box 1005	826-6219
Hanalei, HI 96714	
Paliuli Cottages	8 units
P.O. Box 351	826-6264
Hanalei, HI 96714	
Sandpiper Village One	58 units
P.O. Box 460	826-9613
Hanalei, HI 96714	
Hanalei Colony Resort	48 units
Hanalei, HI 96714	826-6235

Hotels in Poipu

Garden Isle Beach Cottages	7 units
R.R. 1, Box 355	742-6717
Koloa, HI 96756	
Kiahuna Plantation	333 units
R.R. 1, Box 73	742-6411
Koloa, HI 96756	
The Makahuena	742-9555
1661 Pee Road	
Koloa, HI 96756	

Hotels in Poipu (Continued)

Koloa Landing Cottages	3 units
R.R. 1, Box 70	742-14
Koloa, HI 96756	
Nihi Kai Villas	36 unit
1870 Hoone Road	742-64
Koloa, HI 96756	
Lawai Beach Resort	742-95
5017 Lawai Road	
Koloa, HI 96756	
Poipu Kai	98 unit
P.O. Box 173	742-64
Koloa, HI 96756	
Poipu Kapili Condominiums	41 unit
R.R. 1, Box 272	742-64
Koloa, HI 96756	
Poipu Beach Hotel	142 un
Koloa, HI 96756	742-16
Poipu Shores Resort Condominium	35 unit
R.R. 1, Box 95	742-65
Koloa, HI 96756	
Sheraton Kauai Hotel	222 un
Rt. 1, Box 303	742-16
Koloa, HI 96756	
Poipu Crater	742-74
2330 Hoohu Road	
Koloa, HI 96756	
Sunset Kahili Condominium Apts.	26 unit
R.R. 1, Box 96	742-16
Koloa, HI 96756	
Waiohai Hotel	435 un
P.O. Box 174	742-95
Koloa, HI 96756	
Prince Kuhio Resort	45 unit
R.R. 1,	752-16
Koloa, HI 96756	

Hotels — Lihue to Kokee

Kahili Mountain Park	8 units (cabin
P.O. Box 298	742-9921
Koloa, HI 96756	

Kokee Lodge
P.O. Box 819
Waimea, HI 96796

12 cabins
335-6061

Hotels in Waimea

Waimea Plantation Cottages
P.O. Box 367
Waimea, HI 96796

338-1625

Restaurants in Lihue

J.J.'s Broiler
2971 Haleko Road
245-3841

Dinner
Steakhouse

Tip Top Cafe
3173 Akahi St.
245-2333

Breakfast, lunch, dinner
Oriental, American

Pizza Hut
3171 Kuhio Hwy
245-9531

Lunch, dinner
Italian, American

Barbecue Inn
Kress St.
245-2921

Breakfast, lunch, dinner
Japanese, American

Lihue Cafe & Chop Sui
2978 Umi
245-6471

Dinner
Oriental

Restaurant Kiibo
Umi Street
245-2650

Lunch, dinner
Japanese

Rggberts
4481 Rice
245-9025

Breakfast, lunch
American

Casa Italiana
Haleko Road
245-9586

Dinner
Italian

Ho's Garden
3016 Umi
245-5255

Lunch, dinner
Chinese

Dani's Restaurant
4201 Rice
245-4991

Breakfast, lunch
Hawaiian, Japanese

Tomi's
4252 Rice
245-8792

Breakfast, lunch
American

Ma's Family
4277 Halenani
245-3142

Breakfast, lunch
Hawaiian, American

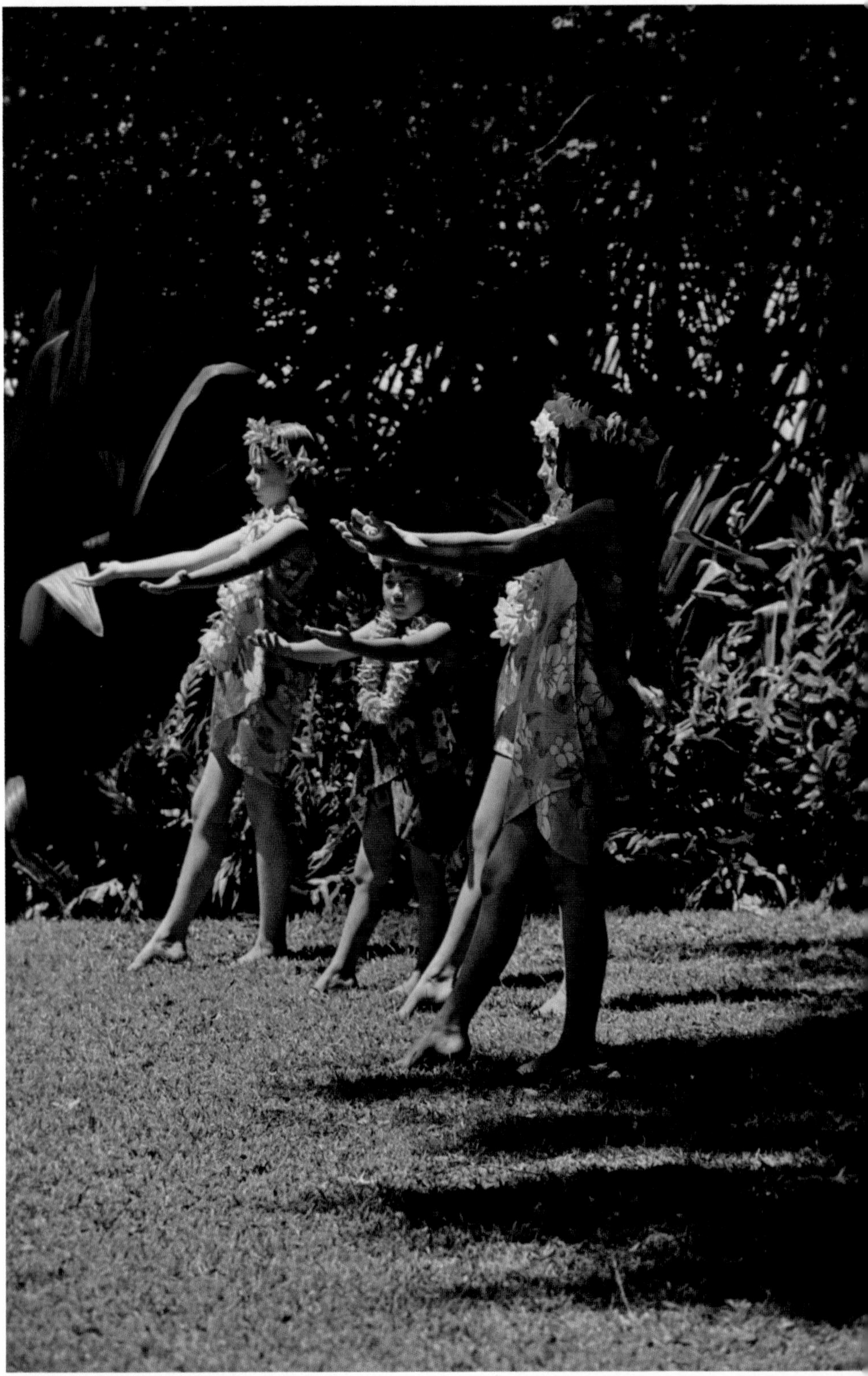

Restaurants Near Lihue

Club Jetty Nawiliwili Harbor 245-4970	Dinner Oriental, Hawaiian
Oar House Nawiliwili 245-4941	Dinner American
The Bull Shed Harbor Village 245-4551	Dinner Steak, seafood
Denmar's Harbor Village 245-3917	Breakfast, lunch, dinner Mexican, American
Kauai Chop Suey Harbor Village 245-8790	Lunch, dinner Chinese
Rosita's Kukui Grove Center 245-8561	Lunch, dinner Mexican
Kukui Nut Tree Inn Kukui Grove Center 245-7005	Breakfast, lunch, dinner American
Brick Oven Pizza Kukui Grove Center 245-1895	Lunch, dinner Italian
Carriage House Restaurant Kilohana 245-9593	Dinner American
Gaylords Kilohana 245-9593	Lunch, dinner American

Restaurants — Lihue to Kapaa
(along Highway 56)

Hanamaulu Restaurant & Tea House Hanamaulu 245-2511	Lunch, dinner Oriental
Mile Two Restaurant Hanamaulu 245-1606	Lunch, dinner American
Fairway Restaurant Wailua Golf Course 245-3451	Breakfast, lunch American, Oriental
Wailua Marina Restaurant Wailua Marina 822-1128	Breakfast, lunch, dinner American, Oriental

Sea Shell Restaurant Wailua 822-3632	Dinner Seafood
Sizzler Wailua 822-7404	Breakfast, lunch, dinner Steak, seafood
Kintaro Restaurant Wailua 822-3341	Dinner Japanese
J.J.'s Boiler Room The Market Place 822-4411	Dinner Steakhouse
Jolly Roger The Market Place 822-3451	Breakfast, lunch, dinner American
Buzz's Steak and Lobster The Market Place 822-7491	Breakfast, lunch, dinner Steak, seafood
Ramona's Restaurant The Market Place 822-5919	Lunch, dinner Mexican
Atami Restaurant Waipouli 822-1642	Lunch, dinner Japanese
The Bullshed Waipouli 822-3791	Dinner Steak, seafood
Dragon Inn Waipouli 822-3788	Lunch, dinner Chinese
Aloha Diner Waipouli 822-3851	Lunch, dinner Hawaiian

Restaurants — Kapaa to Haena
(along Highway 56)

Norberto's El Cafe Kapaa 822-3362	Lunch, dinner Mexican
Ono Family Restaurant Kapaa 822-1710	Breakfast, lunch, dinner American
Rib n' Tail Kapaa 822-9632	Dinner Steak, seafood
Kountry Kitchen Kapaa 822-3511	Breakfast, lunch, dinner American

Kapaa Fish & Chowder House Kapaa 822-7488	Lunch, dinner Steak, seafood
Casa di Amici Kilauea 828-1388	Lunch, dinner Italian
The Flats Grill & Bar Princeville 826-7255	Lunch, dinner Cajun, American
The Oasis Princeville 826-1449	Lunch, dinner Natural food
Chuck's Steak House Princeville 826-6211	Lunch, dinner Steak, seafood
Beamreach Restaurant Princeville 826-9131	Dinner Steak, seafood
Shell House Hanalei 826-7977	Breakfast, lunch, dinner American
Tahiti Nui Hanalei 826-6277	Lunch, dinner Hawaiian, American
Foong Wong Hanalei 826-7434	Lunch, dinner Chinese
Dolphin Restaurant Hanalei 826-6113	Dinner Steak, seafood
Charo's Haena 826-6422	Lunch, dinner Steak, seafood
Papagayo Haena 826-9442	Lunch, dinner Mexican

Restaurants in Poipu

Koloa Broiler Koloa 742-9122	Lunch, dinner American
Koloa Fish & Chowder House Koloa 742-7377	Lunch, dinner Seafood
Plantation Gardens Poipu 742-1695	Dinner Seafood

Aquarium Restaurant   Dinner
Poipu   Italian
742-9505

Beach House Restaurant   Dinner
Poipu   Steak, seafood
742-7575

Brenneckes Beach Broiler   Lunch, dinner
Poipu   Steak, seafood
742-7588

Keoki's Paradise   Dinner
Poipu   Steak, seafood
742-7534

Kiahuna Golf Village   Lunch, dinner
Poipu   American
742-6055

Restaurants — Lihue to Kekaha
(along Highway 50)

Brick Oven Pizza   Lunch, dinner
Kalaheo   Italian
332-8561

Kalaheo Restaurant   Lunch, dinner
Kalaheo   American
332-9755

Kauai Kim Chee   Dinner
Kalaheo   Korean
332-8336

Green Garden Restaurant   Breakfast, lunch, dinner
Hanapepe   Oriental, Hawaiian, American
335-5422

Leeward Diner   Breakfast, lunch
Hanapepe   Hawaiian, Oriental
335-5231

Conrad's   Breakfast, lunch, dinner
Hanapepe   Oriental
335-5066

Kauai Kitchen   Breakfast, lunch
Hanapepe   American
335-6170

Linda's Restaurant   Breakfast, lunch
Hanapepe   Oriental, American
355-5152

Wrangler's Restaurant   Lunch, dinner
Waimea   American
338-1266

Traveler's Den   Lunch, dinner
Kekaha   American
337-9922

Restaurants in Kokee

Kokee Lodge Restaurant   Lunch
Kokee State Park   American
335-6061

Annual Events

February – Capt. Cook Caper in Waimea. First weekend after Presidents Day. Parade/ food/entertainment/booths.

March – Prince Kuhio Festical. Islandwide week of festivities. State Holiday honoring Kuhio. Parade/royal ball.

May – Kauai Museum Lei Day Contest. Museum fills with the most exquisite and fragrant leis made by people of all ages.

June – King Kamehameha Celebration. Statewide celebration. Parade and special events.

July – Koloa Plantation Days. Annual celebration of more than 150 years of sugar. Parade/mill tours/historic celebration.

August – End of Summer Beach Party in Waimea. Old fashioned daylong luau/games/ entertainment.

Pooku Annual Hanlei Stampede. Statewide rodeo/music/dancing.

September – Kauai County Fair. Exhibits/produce/flowers/4H entertainment/rides.

October – Kauai Loves You Triathalon

December – Kauai Museum Christmas Fair – the best in island crafts.

Menehune Fishpond

Sailing off Poipu Beach

Kiahuna Beach and Tennis Resort Pool

Fern Grotto

Hanakapiai

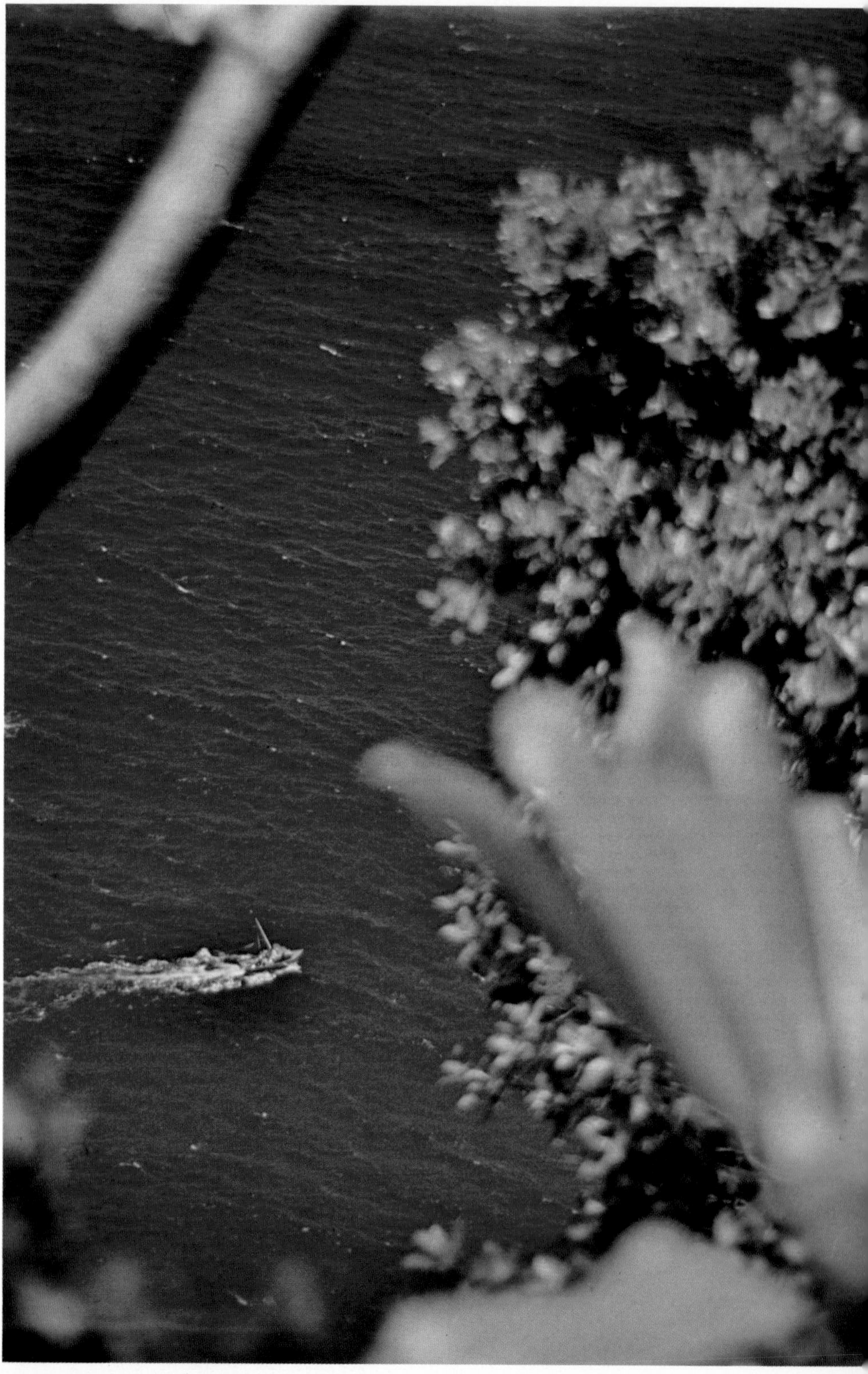

Island of KAUAI

POINTS OF INTEREST

1 Kauai Museum
2 Lutheran Church
3 Westin Kauai
4 Menehune Gardens
5 Menehune Fishpond
6 Plantation Gardens
7 Prince Kuhio's Birthplace
8 Spounting Horn
9 Kukuiolono Park
10 Pacific Tropical Botanical Garden
11 Salt Pond
12 Fort Elizabeth (or Russian Fort)
13 Menehune Ditch
14. Waimea Canyon Lookout
15 Kokee State Park
16 Kalalau lookout
17 Barking Sands
18 Polihale Park
19 Wailua Falls
20 Fern Grotto
21 Smith's Tropical Paradise
22 Opaekaa Falls
23 Kilauea Slippery Slides
24 Kilauea Lighthouse
25 Waioli Mission House
26 Hanalei Bay
27 Lumahai Beach
28 Dry Cave
29 Wet Cave
30 Kee Beach

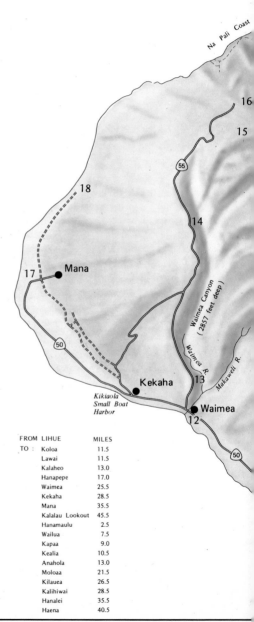

FROM LIHUE	MILES
TO : Koloa	11.5
Lawai	11.5
Kalaheo	13.0
Hanapepe	17.0
Waimea	25.5
Kekaha	28.5
Mana	35.5
Kalalau Lookout	45.5
Hanamaulu	2.5
Wailua	7.5
Kapaa	9.0
Kealia	10.5
Anahola	13.0
Moloaa	21.5
Kilauea	26.5
Kalihiwai	28.5
Hanalei	35.5
Haena	40.5

0   2   4   6   8
Miles

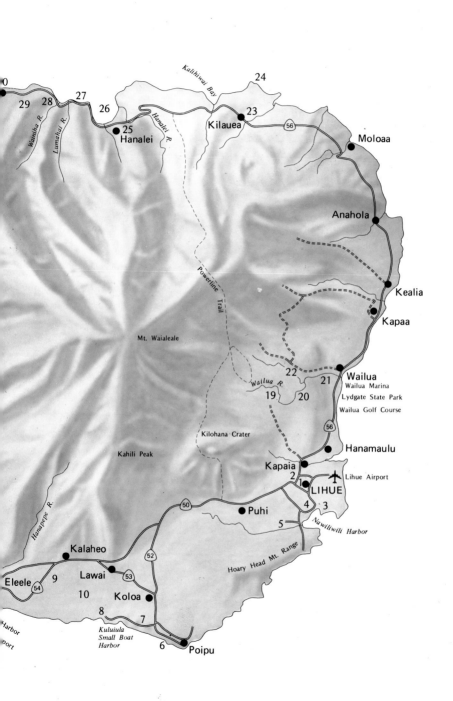

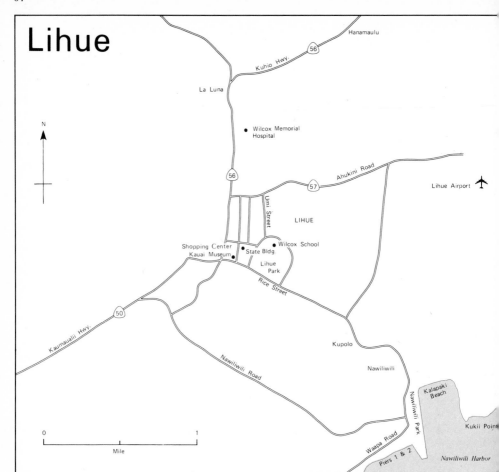

Lihue

Hanamaulu

Kuhio Hwy. 56

La Luna

N

● Wilcox Memorial Hospital

Ahukini Road

56

57

Lihue Airport

Umi Street

LIHUE

Shopping Center ● Wilcox School
Kauai Museum ● ● State Bldg.

Lihue Park

Rice Street

50

Kaumualii Hwy.

Kupolo

Nawiliwili Road

Nawiliwili

Nawiliwili Park

Kalapaki Beach

Kukii Point

0   1
Mile

Waapa Road

Piers 1 & 2

Nawiliwili Harbor

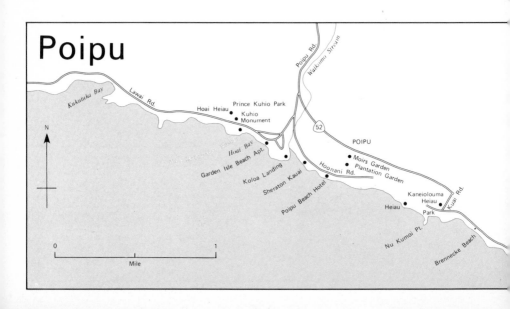

Poipu

Poipu Rd.

Waikomo Stream

Kukuiula Bay

Lawai Rd.

Hoai Heiau

Prince Kuhio Park

Kuhio Monument

N

52

POIPU

Hoai Bay

Garden Isle Beach Apt.

Koloa Landing

Sheraton Kauai

Moirs Garden
Plantation Garden

Hoonani Rd.

Poipu Beach Hotel

Kaneiolouma Heiau

Kuai Rd.

Heiau

Park

0   1
Mile

Nu Kumoi Pt.

Brennecke Beach